Between a Rock

and a Camera Lens

The Finn Class in Photos at the
Rio 2016 Olympic Sailing Competition

Robert Deaves

Published by Robert Deaves, 2017

First Edition 2017

ISBN 978-0-9559001-6-7

Copyright © Robert Deaves, 2017

A CIP catalogue record for this book is available from the British Library.

BETWEEN A ROCK

AND A CAMERA LENS

MORE THAN 400 PHOTOS FROM THE RIO 2016 OLYMPIC GAMES

ROBERT DEAVES

CONTENTS

INTRODUCTION

The 2016 Olympic Sailing Competition was all it was anticipated and headlined to be – and a lot more besides. The talk going into the regatta was that anything and everything could happen. It certainly lived up to that billing, but unexpectedly the whole regatta, for Finns at least, went to schedule, barring the occasional wait for the wind. Despite the early gloomy forecasts of predominantly light winds, there was a good mix of everything, light days and windy days, flat water and huge waves, sunshine and storms. No one could say the conditions favoured any one sailor in particular.

Sailors spent longer training at the venue than at any previous Olympics, many starting three years previously to familiarise themselves with the conditions and many based themselves there for protracted periods to get to grips with Rio's idiosyncrasies. Most were fully aware it wouldn't take much for everything to go horribly wrong for them.

Before the start of racing, what all the sailors were saying, whatever their past results would otherwise indicate, was that this would be an Olympics where past form meant very little. They all knew these Games would be very tough to manage, and very difficult to predict, and to win you had to be the best all round sailor - and perhaps a little lucky.

The fleet of 23 sailors included two former medalists from London 2012 - Jonas Høgh-Christensen and Jonathan Lobert,

the European Champion Pieter-Jan Postma, and the four-time World Champion Giles Scott, who was the absolute favourite to take gold, having won all but two regattas over the previous three years.

Scott didn't make it easy on himself with a number of uncharacteristic errors, but by the end of the week he was never going to be beaten for gold. The venue proved tricky and unpredictable, catching him out on a number of occasions, most notably in the opening race when he had a fight on just to finish 17th. After that it was sublime sailing for the four-time world champion, with just one more race outside the top 10, and eight times in the top three. Even if all the predictions were for him to win, it was still a surprise, even to him, that he managed to achieve it in quite the manner he did. Perhaps this is an accurate reflection of Scott's calm and casual style: no stress, no drama, just get the job done in the most efficient way.

Vasilij Žbogar's dream was to end his remarkable Olympic career with a third medal, after a silver and bronze medals in the Laser class. He was the oldest Finn sailor in Rio and felt the demands of Rio on his body more than most of the fleet, but his experience paid off and the silver medal was a fitting reward for the effort he had put in over six years in the class. He put in one of his best ever performances, consistent in the light winds and just hanging on in the breeze to minimise the points. His reaction at winning silver was priceless – disbelief mixed with delight.

Compared to the other two medalists, Caleb Paine had an inconsistent week, dramatically survived a potentially decisive protest, and then, despite several high scores rallied towards the end of the week to put himself right back into contention for a medal. Regardless of the ups and downs he held his

composure and concentration right to the end. His confident win in the medal race put the bronze almost beyond doubt from the first mark.

In the end it was a tough, challenging week in Rio for the Finn class. Most of the 'favourites' failed to live up to expectations and many failed to even make the medal race. This speaks volumes about Rio as a venue, but more importantly about the competitive depth within the Finn class. The racing was as tight as the class had ever seen, with just metres separating many boats after an hour of racing, the complex conditions stretching every sailor through the light days as well as the epic, monumental days at sea with monster waves. But all along, one man was perhaps destined to dominate and come away with the gold medal.

Sailing a Finn is a demanding occupation. Every one of the 23 Finn sailors who made it to Rio made huge sacrifices to be there and many went home with unrealised goals and unfulfilled ambition. Some will be back, some won't, but all will have a unique bond with a sporting event that played out as one of the tightest, closest, and most challenging Olympic regattas ever.

The 2016 Olympics for the Finn class was an absorbing battle of wits, skill, strength and mental stamina. The three worthy medalists highlighted the diversity of sailors and the skill sets required to conquer the Finn as well as Rio's challenging conditions. Caleb Paine, brimming with young ambition, hard work and a sense of optimism; Vasilij Žbogar, the veteran of five Olympics, with huge experience and skill, and still not quite believing he had achieved his dream ending; and Giles Scott the undisputed king of Finn sailing in the quadrennium.

The 23 Finn athletes in Rio were the youngest, fittest, strongest and tallest group of Finn sailors ever assembled at an Olympic Games. The line-up included seven former World or European Champions, six former Junior Champions and four former Olympic medalists (two in the Finn, one in the Star and one in the Laser).

Of the 23, just seven were sailing their first Olympics, seven were sailing their second, five were sailing their third, two were sailing their fourth and two were sailing their fifth: Vasilij Žbogar and Allan Julie. Facundo Olezza was the youngest at 21, while Žbogar was the oldest at 40, and the average age was 29, down one year from London 2012. The sailors ranged from 88 to 102 kg in weight and from 1.81 to 2.04 metres in height.

Looking at it qualitatively, based on earlier performance, about 10-12 sailors could be said to have had the capacity to medal, and around 18-20 had performed well enough to make the medal race. In spite of all the form predictions, several favourites failed to perform and the final results paints an interesting picture of diverse conditions and inconsistency.

**FACUNDO OLEZZA
ARGENTINA**

**JAKE LILLEY
AUSTRALIA**

**JORGE ZARIF
BRAZIL**

**TOM RAMSHAW
CANADA**

**LEI GONG
CHINA**

**IVAN
KLJAKOVIĆ GAŠPIĆ
CROATIA**

**JONAS HØGH-
CHRISTENSEN
DENMARK**

**DENISS KARPAK
ESTONIA**

**TAPIO NIRRKO
FINLAND**

**JONATHAN LOBERT
FRANCE**

**GILES SCOTT
GREAT BRITAIN**

**IOANNIS MITAKIS
GREECE**

**ZSOMBOR BERECZ
HUNGARY**

**GIORGIO POGGI
ITALY**

**PIETER-JAN
POSTMA
NETHERLANDS**

**JOSH JUNIOR
NEW ZEALAND**

**ANDERS
PEDERSEN
NORWAY**

**ALLAN JULIE
SEYCHELLES**

**VASILIJ ŽBOGAR
SLOVENIA**

**MAX SALMINEN
SWEDEN**

**ALICAN KAYNAR
TURKEY**

**ALEJANDRO
FOGLIA
URUGUAY**

**CALEB PAINE
USA**

The opening day was a day in which many of the favourites saw a different end of the fleet than expected. Sailed under the Sugarloaf mountain it was always going to be the hardest day of the week, but no one expected it to be as hard as it was. It was a day full of shocks as the fleet suffered 40 degree shifts and pressure changes that mixed the order on almost every leg.

The youngest sailor, Facundo Olezza won the first race, while the oldest sailor, Vasilij Žbogar won the second. Alican Kaynar was the early leader in Race 1 before Deniss Karpak took the lead downwind after a huge shift turned the first run into a reach. Olezza was next in the lead on the following downwind to lead through to the finish from Kaynar and Žbogar.

"If you asked someone if they are OK with a fourth and sixth, then on a normal day some guys would say no, but on a day like today it's two good results. On the Sugarloaf race area it's the worst one to keep a good average."
– Jorge Zarif

"The fleet is really strong and everybody is very close, so making small mistakes can lose you five to ten places very easily."
– Vasilij Žbogar

"The Sugarloaf course is notoriously difficult...the breeze comes straight down over Sugarloaf, which provides really tricky, unpredictable winds."
– Giles Scott

The second race was sailed in slightly more stable winds, at least in terms of pressure but still lacking in any particular direction. Žbogar held a nice lead at the top after favouring the left, but on the second upwind, Zsombor Berecz went right and popped out ahead, while Žbogar covered the majority on the left.

However, the Hungarian, along with Josh Junior, Jake Lilley and Alejandro Foglia were all pulled out after a starting penalty to leave Žbogar the winner from Jonas Høgh-Christensen and Giles Scott.

After the first day, Žbogar held a three point lead over Kaynar and a six point lead over Olezza. However the story of the day was the poor start from the favourite, Giles Scott.

"We knew the left was much better but with this place you never know actually."
– Vasilij Žbogar

"We knew it was going to be tricky on this course and there was a good chance that we would have some randomness in races, and we sure did."
– Jonas Høgh Christensen

"I'm not massively happy with how today has gone, but there is still a long way to go. It's certainly not the way you want to start an Olympic Games but unfortunately these things happen in regattas, and they have certainly happened to me over the past four years, so it doesn't make things easy."
– Giles Scott

Racing off Niterói on the ocean, the Finn fleet excelled in the huge waves and big winds. Giles Scott put his first day worries behind him to win the day and move into the overall lead. The conditions were full on. With a persistent rain, a strong, cold wind, and big, breaking waves catching out the unwary, the lights along Copacabana shone brightly through the murk. It was definitely not the Rio in the brochure, but the Finn sailors loved it all the same. Ioannis Mitakis led round the top mark in the first race of the day after some confusion in the bad visibility over the marks. Zsombor Berecz took the lead downwind, but then Jonathan Lobert, who had rounded third, moved ahead on the second upwind to lead into the finish from Scott and Mitakis. Four sailors later requested redress after heading to the wrong set of windward marks, but to no avail.

"It was incredibly windy, top end that we would be racing in. 20-25 knots, big seas, made for really full on racing, but to come away with a second and a first is a lot more pleasing than my day yesterday."
– Giles Scott

"I was near the front in the first one, and I was struggling a bit with speed but also with placing. You need to be in the shift, and in the gust. With the last race I was in the game. I need to build on that. The results are all over the place. It is hard but it doesn't matter if it's hard, as if it's hard it's challenging and that's good."

– Pieter-Jan Postma

"I think the four races so far show two things, the level of the fleet and how difficult the conditions are here...it's tough as everyone is on peak form and racing really well. That provides its challenges but it's really enjoyable."
– Jake Lilley

"It was a nice breeze for the Finns. I had two really good races. Normally I am not in the top three in these conditions but I knew that I had good speed, so I knew I had to have good starts and then you are out of the pack."
– Ioannis Mitakis

Giles Scott went one better in Race 4, to lead at every mark to win by 50 seconds. Ioannis Mitakis again produced an outstanding performance in the challenging conditions to cross second, while Caleb Paine made up for a poor first race with a third place finish. After all that, Scott took the lead, Vasilij Žbogar dropped to second, and Alican Kaynar dropped one place to third.

"I didn't really have my best groove on and got a little bit of the phasing wrong early in both races but managed to grind away and get two keepers."

– Jake Lilley

"It's incredibly changeable. We've spent an awful lot of days here, so to get conditions you've never seen before, like today, is pretty unlikely. I guess that's just Rio."

– Giles Scott

"I was happy with the first race. My speed was good and I managed to sail well and won. The second race I was leading again but I didn't look enough and lost everything. So mixed feelings today."
– Jonathan Lobert

"I pulled the clew ring out of the back of my sail so the sail is destroyed, which is a bit unfortunate. So I had to retire. It was pretty crazy out there, 25-30 knots and big waves. It was great for the Finn, awesome conditions; I wish this was what was on TV. "
– Jonas Høgh-Christensen

The third day was a spectacular day of sailing with big winds, huge seas and even bigger stakes.

A change to the schedule put the fleet on the Copacabana course area outside the bay. With the wind pushing past 25 knots, and 2 to 3 metres waves, on an even larger swell coming down the course, it was no day to be shy. Giles Scott moved into an 11-point lead with Vasilij Žbogar fighting hard to hang onto second. Zsombor Berecz moved up the fleet to third after a great day.

In the first race, Jorge Zarif knew where he was going and led round the top mark from the right corner. But Berecz was not far behind and took the lead on the second upwind to take the win from Zarif and Tapio Nirkko. Scott made a crucial mistake and was too far back to catch the leaders.

"...the greatest day in my sailing career. I can't be happier than this. I was a bit disappointed in the morning when they moved us from the inside course to the outside. We knew it would be windy and choppy again today as we expected more wind and bigger waves. But as we were on Copacabana we only had the waves coming from one direction so it was more manageable than yesterday. I had a great first race. We had a plan. We executed it, and it worked, because I won the race."
– Zsombor Berecz

"I think the secret today was to find a good line to cross to the right and I had a good line and good boat speed and I was lucky to cross fully to the right. And that's it. Less current, and more wind. And then in the second one I tried to tack as soon as could after the start, but I was too late already."
– Jorge Zarif

"I knew I would struggle in strong wind. In my mind I knew that I had to get as less points as possible."
– Vasilij Žbogar

"It was a fun day. You can't ask for better sailing conditions really. That was the ultimate conditions for sailing a Finn. I was happy with my first race. In the second race I slowed down a bit but still happy how I sailed."
– Tom Ramshaw

Race 6 followed a similar pattern to race 5 with perhaps slightly more wind and slightly larger waves. This time, Giles Scott, got it right and, after passing Jake Lilley on the first downwind, led round the rest of the course for an impressive win.

Caleb Paine finally crossed second, with Josh Junior securing third.

"It was a really breezy day with big waves out there. I managed to change a few things and finally got my boat going a bit faster and sailed a lot better, so I'm stoked."
– Josh Junior

"We have four more tough races and for sure it's going to be light, which I am happy about because I am quite tired now. My dream is getting close. We will not change anything; we will just keep the routine."
– Zsombor Berecz

"And the good thing is in this game you are not alone, so I was lucky that the others were also making mistakes in the strong winds. I was a bit lucky on my side that the others didn't use their strength in their conditions."
– Vasilij Žbogar

"I think the important thing to remember is that everyone has big scores now. I don't think there is one person who has been massively consistent so you really have to fight for every single position, no matter where you find yourself.
There is still a long way to go and it's going to be tough."
– Giles Scott

"A medal is a lot on now. I'm just trying to get as much up the fleet as possible, race as many good races as possible and see what happens from there."
– Josh Junior

Giles Scott exerted his control over the fleet as the Finns returned to the water after a lay day. Instead of the scheduled sea course, the fleet was sent to the furthest inshore by the Guanabara Bay road bridge. The day belonged to Scott, Vasilij Žbogar and Jake Lilley, the only sailors to get two good results. But the racing was incredibly close. After 50 minutes of full-on racing, these world-class athletes were separated by just seconds. No one gave an inch.

The right-hand side was clearly the preferred choice, but the reality was subtly different with gains to be made on the left and the middle. Lilley led round the top mark in Race 7, but Scott soon took the lead downwind to extend for the win. Behind him it was very close. The biggest mover was Jorge Zarif coming through from 15th at the top to second at the final downwind mark to lead Lilley into the finish by a few seconds.

"It's been very hard. I have lived and sailed here for 15 years and sometimes I don't know what goes on here. It's hard to predict."

– Jorge Zarif

"The level is extremely high and you have to push all the time. It's nice from my side because it is really close racing and it's tough, but it's exhausting as well."
– Vasilij Žbogar

"We had a different day compared to the last few days. Very tight tactical racing and it was good to put some low scores together. Everyone has big scores, so anything can happen."

– Jake Lilley

"Rio really delivered some great conditions for us. Nice clear skies, the sea breeze kicked in, the wind funnelled straight down the bay, with a nice and clean 12 knots. Really nice sailing. It's nice to put in consistent results at the top of the fleet. I think myself and Vasilij had a good day today and behind that there were a few guys that were up and down."
– Giles Scott

"It's exciting and the competition is fierce. Everyone is performing well and the differences are minor. We can only see Giles a bit in front, and Vasilij is quite consistent. Everyone has high expectations and we are all pushing really hard but at such a level you can always make a few mistakes. It's the same for me."
– Ivan Kljakovic Gaspic

Race 8 was almost as close at Race 7, with Jonas Høgh-Christensen finding the top mark first after favouring the left side of the course, but it all went horribly wrong from there on, losing 15 places before the finish.

Pieter-Jan Postma rounded the top mark in second place and took the lead on the first downwind, never to be threatened for the win.

Josh Junior was the biggest climber, finally finding his form, and coming through from 11th at the first mark to second at the finish, while Giles Scott extended his lead overall with a third place finish.

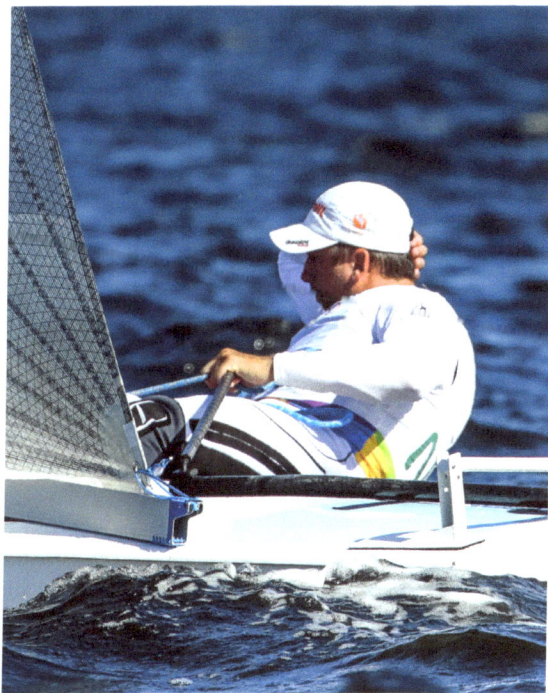

"To make these two results keeps me alive. First I need to get into the medal race."
– Vasilij Žbogar

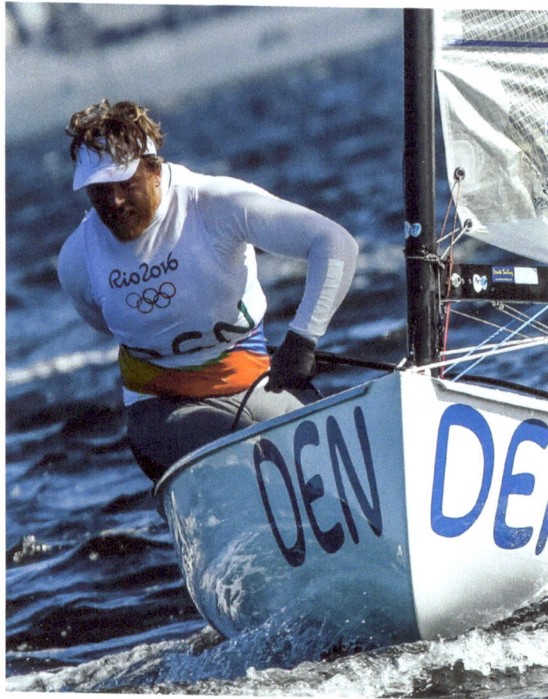

"The races are very close. Everyone is now good on the downwind, as opposed to a few years ago. Also everyone has a lot of different results. The important thing is to be close to the top guys going into the last day."
– Jorge Zarif

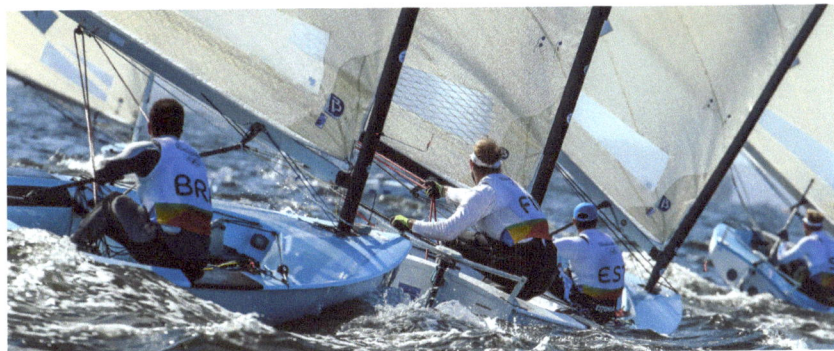

"What is incredible is how compact the fleet is, how we are battling for half a metre. Before we were battling for 10 metres, now it is less than one metre. And we all crossed the finish in a minute. This has never happened before in the Finn class."
– Vasilij Žbogar

"It's amazingly close racing. The first downwind I won three or four places, the second I lost 10. And the last two I extended. And at the mark roundings everyone was super close."
– Pieter-Jan Postma

"Having the points margin is a big confidence booster, but the thing for me to focus on is that it isn't over, you can't get complacent, you need to attack tomorrow, like I've done today."
– Giles Scott

Giles Scott sealed the gold medal early after two more light wind races off Niterói. Again, Rio's challenging conditions provided a mixed bag of results, with several sailors picking up high scores. With no clear form through the fleet apart from Scott and Vasilij Žbogar, it was always going to be a scrap to the finish, with the points around the medal race cut off very close. For the fifth day in a row it was all change once again.

After a long postponement, first ashore and then afloat to wait for the wind, Ivan Kljakovic Gaspic, who ended the day third overall, started by leading round the top mark in Race 9, in very light winds. He was passed on the second upwind by Facundo Olezza who maintained the lead all the way to the finish. Alejandro Foglia, who had rounded the top mark in 15th, found some speed to cross in third.

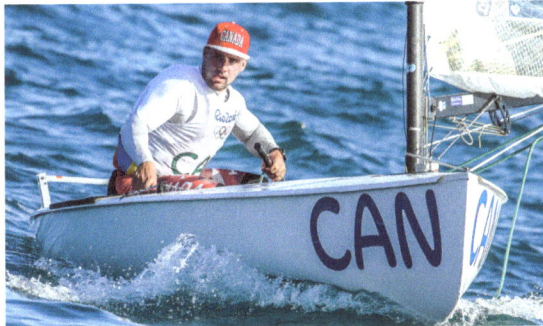

"I am really happy just to be here and competing for a medal after a quite long way, and progressing after four years. It's cool to be here. I am happy with my progress through the week. It took a while to get into it and really find a focus and drive in the boat. Since then it's only gone better and better. The years training here have certainly helped, especially on Saturday and Sunday where we got conditions that we were more expecting."

– Max Salminen

"The first race was quite light, but for me was regular. There were big differences in the downwind in pressure and positions so it was not easy to sail. I was lucky being extended on the front so I didn't have this headache, but for other guys it was quite tough."

– Ivan Kljakovic Gaspic

"In the first race if there were not the big waves, it would have been easy sailable, but the waves made it almost impossible. It was up and down and was a bit of a lottery at the end. Many guys were ahead and lost everything."
– Vasilij Žbogar

"It feels weird. I work a lot but I'm new to the class so I was not expecting too much from this. I don't know how I'm feeling. This is new for me. This feels great, but it's weird."

– Facundo Olezza

After struggling with his form all week, Alejandro Foglia won the final day by winning Race 10 after overtaking Giles Scott on the final downwind. Caleb Paine had rounded first but dropped to fourth while Ioannis Mitakis crossed in third.

To make sure of the gold with a day to spare, Scott needed three points on Žbogar. In the first race, he lost ground on the second upwind and finished just one place ahead. In the final race, Scott needed to be just two boats ahead of Žbogar. For a while they were very close, but after few errors from Žbogar on the second upwind Scott escaped, and the gold was his.

A last place for Lilley in Race 9 dropped him out of the medal race, after starting the day in third, but after Pieter-Jan Postma was disqualified from Race 10 for a start line penalty, Lilley gained one point to overtake Mitakis and was back in the medal race.

"It was a really difficult day, really stressful because the wind was up and down. Puffs of wind were all over the race area and it was impossible to predict, so very tough mentally. I tried to be conservative playing the middle, and I lost a few places there in both races. But at the end I think I managed to have two good races, which was really good in these conditions."
– Vasilij Žbogar

"There have been a lot of ups and downs but it's always good to finish on a great day. There is still a lot of racing to be had in the medal race and I'm just looking forward to finishing it off and hopefully getting a medal."
– Caleb Paine

"If you'd have asked me, would I have won the Olympic Games before the medal race, I'd have said absolutely not because of the venue that it is. It's such a privileged situation to be in because for everybody else who is going to be fighting it out for those medals; it's going to be incredibly stressful and to be able to say I'm not going to have to go through that is pretty nice."

– Giles Scott

"We expected mixed conditions and we got very mixed conditions. Maybe surprisingly mixed actually but all in all, a little bit like we expected."
– Max Salminen

"I can't quite believe that I've managed to put together the regatta I have."
– Giles Scott

Giles Scott still had to sail the medal race, but the result for him was irrelevant. Mathematically, any boat in the top 10 could win a medal, and while Vasilij Žbogar was almost secure for a medal, Caleb Paine or Max Salminen were the greatest threats to third placed Ivan Kljakovic Gaspic.

While most sailors favoured the left side of the upwind, Paine saw some pressure to the right and was rewarded with a monster shift into the first mark that gave him a 30 second jump on the fleet. He cruised away to an easy victory.

Žbogar just had to make sure he was not last. He rounded the top mark in eighth, close on Gaspic's stern, but passed him downwind to eventually cross the finish in sixth to take the bronze.

"I knew if I got ahead and won the race, things would become a lot easier. I was fortunate to establish a lead ahead of time. It's pretty awesome, it's been a pretty tough regatta and to be able to come away with a medal is a great feeling."

– Caleb Paine

"I feel relieved that it's over. It just went well. I was only dreaming of it one week ago. I had nothing to gain in the race; I had everything to lose. Second place for me is something unbelievable."

– Vasilij Žbogar

"It was great to be able to go out and enjoy that race today. Winning four World Championships is great, but this is one that everyone wants and everyone remembers, so now to have an Olympic gold is a great feeling."
– Giles Scott

POSTSCRIPT

Capturing the Finn class on camera at the Rio Olympics was an unforgettable experience. Like the sailors, the week had its ups and downs, but the photos in the book are testament to the fact that Rio has many moods. Every day was different, the backdrops changed, the light changed. On one day the weather was so bad, the only bright points were the lights along Copacabana twinkling through the murk.

Having worked with Olympic Finn sailors for the best part of 25 years it was an eye-opener to see what happens at this level, how the sailors coped with the constant media attention, and how they dealt with unexpected success or failure with the whole world watching closely.

Each day was first spent trying to get a place on board one of the photo boats provided by the organisers, and then making sure the driver got to the right place at the right time to get the photos. Some boats were clearly not up to the job, especially offshore, with everything getting a thorough soaking.

As well as the normal yachting journalists there were also journalists from global news agencies assigned to sailing for the odd day, who had no idea of what to expect. Most went blithely out to sea in all conditions with little or no waterproof protection for either themselves or their expensive camera equipment. Several spent the day in misery with seasickness, and on the third day, on the Copacabana course area, one was even knocked unconscious when he fell over after the boat launched off a big wave.

Like a true professional he apologised to the other photographers because we had missed a mark rounding while trying to raise his lifeless body from the deck. Afterwards, on the way in he asked me how I would grade the day in terms of how tough it was as a day covering sailing. He offered 8/10 or 9/10. I said it was more like 3/10. He seemed disconcerted with my assessment, but it had been the kind of day that sailing photographers dream about. It doesn't get much better than 20-25 knots, sunshine, great visibility and light, with a three metre swell with two metre waves on top, all rolling past Copacabana Beach with Corcovado and Sugarloaf as perfect backdrops.

Even though I have watched hundreds of Finn races over the past 15 years, it was still an immense privilege to watch the Finn racing close up every day in Rio. Having watched Giles calmly win four world championships, this gold was different: the culmination of nine years hard work.

He crossed the line with his head in his hands; the press boats waiting expectantly for him to do something, a display of emotion that would encapsulate his achievement; the mammoth effort to become almost unbeatable. For a while we thought it was business as usual and he wasn't going to react. He made the press wait so long – it was probably only a minute or so – they actually started calling to him to do something. Everyone wanted their photo ops.

Finally he moved. He stood up, threw his arms in the air and let out a huge, unexpected, pent up roar, releasing all the nervous energy of the previous few days. It shattered the tranquil waters off Niterói, as the sun was beginning to set behind Sugarloaf throwing a golden veil over the fleet as they began the long tow back to Marina da Glória. ≈